Lucretia Mott:
Friend of Justice

with a message from
Rosalynn Carter

Written by
Kem Knapp Sawyer

Illustrated by
Leslie Carow

AM I NOT A WOMAN AND A SISTER?

Discovery Enterprises, Ltd., Lowell, Massachusetts

© Discovery Enterprises, Ltd., 1991

ISBN 1-878668-04-8 hard cover/library edition
Library of Congress Catalog Card Number 91-70822

10   9   8   7   6   5   4   3   2   1

Printed in the United States of America

A Word on the Literature

James and Lucretia Mott's Life and Letters was edited by their granddaughter, Anna Davis Hallowell and published by Houghton Mifflin and Company in 1884. It proved invaluable in writing this story. *Lucretia Mott: Her Complete Speeches and Sermons,* edited by Dana Greene (The Edwin Mellen Press, 1980), was also useful. Readers interested in learning more about Lucretia Mott will enjoy Margaret Bacon's *Valiant Friend: The Life of Lucretia Mott* (Walker and Co., 1980) and Otelia Cromwell's *Lucretia Mott* (Harvard University Press, 1958).

Credits

Book design: Jeffrey Pollock. *Typography:* Nancy Myers.
Production: Phyllis Dougherty. *Proofreading and editing:* Andrea L. Weisman.

Subject Reference Guide:

Mott, Lucretia – Biography
Peace Movement – Biography
Society of Friends – Quakers
Underground Railroad
Abolition of Slavery
Women's Rights Movement
Seneca Falls Conference

Acknowledgments

Special thanks to the following for their
help and support in this project:
Jon, Kate, Eve, and Ida Sawyer
Friends Meeting of Washington Library
Friends Historical Library, Swarthmore College
David Ossoff
Barbara Carow
Concord, New Hampshire Public Library

Rosalynn Carter

Lucretia Mott is one of my favorite heroines of the women's rights movement. She was a Quaker, and because of her religious beliefs she was opposed to slavery and war. She also believed that women were equal to men in all respects. These beliefs were not popular in her lifetime.

Lucretia was married and unlike most women at the time, she believed that her marriage did not just join "husband and wife," but two equal partners. She was the mother of six children.

Lucretia taught school and, also, became a Quaker minister. In her middle-fifties she traveled to London to attend a World Anti-Slavery Convention and was shocked to learn that the women who had come so far would not be allowed to speak. When she returned, her anger led her to help organize a women's rights convention at Seneca Falls, New York, in 1848.

Seneca Falls was the first time that a women's rights meeting led to a sustained movement for reform. But it would be over seventy years before women would be allowed to vote in our country.

The reasons I like Lucretia Mott are that she had a balance in her life between family, and religious and political issues. And when she believed strongly in a cause she was willing to work hard to see it through. She lived to be eighty-seven and most of her life was spent speaking out against war, and trying to secure equal rights for both blacks and women.

Lucretia Mott is an excellent role model for children, and I am sure children of all ages will enjoy reading this book about her life.

Rosalynn Carter

Lucretia loved to roast potatoes in the fireplace.

Nantucket Childhood

"Now, after you have finished knitting, you may go down cellar and pick out as many as you want of the smallest potatoes, the very smallest, and roast them in the ashes," Anna Coffin told her children when she had to leave the house. Lucretia loved to roast potatoes in the fireplace—it was one of her favorite treats. On Nantucket, an island thirty miles off the coast of Massachusetts where the Coffins lived, the winters were long and cold. Outside the wind blew and the waves crashed against the shore, but inside the fire made the children feel warm and cozy. There was nothing Lucretia liked better than stirring the coals with a long stick. Years later, long after she had grown up and left her childhood home, she could still recall the taste of the hot and slightly charred potatoes.

Lucretia's parents, Thomas and Anna, both had grown up on Nantucket and were married there. They had six children—five daughters and one son. Lucretia, the second oldest, was born in mid-winter on January 3, 1793, two centuries ago. The way of life on Nantucket then was primitive and those who remained on the island were courageous and energetic. They needed to be strong in mind and body in order to survive. Thomas and Anna were just that. And like so many of Nantucket's inhabitants, they belonged to the Society of Friends, a religion that deeply influenced their lives and their children's lives.

Both Thomas and Anna's ancestors were among the first settlers to arrive on the island in 1659. A few years later they were followed by members of the Society of Friends, also called Quakers because they were said to tremble as they prayed. Like other religious groups, Quakers in England had been mistreated due to their beliefs. They were often arrested and hundreds died in prisons. Many came to the New World hoping to find religious freedom. But even in the New World they were sometimes persecuted. Between 1659 and 1661 Boston witnessed the execution of four Quakers. But on Nantucket Quakers felt secure and could enjoy the freedom to practice their own religion. They also found that land was cheap and they could afford to build homes.

Thomas took to the sea to make a living.

The island seamen captured whales and extracted oil from them. They took the oil from the whale's fat, which is called "blubber," and used it to light lamps and to make soap and candles. These whalers were so successful that Nantucket became the most profitable whaling center in the New World. Following the island tradition, Thomas took to the sea to make a living. Trading and whaling frequently took him away from home. He sailed on long voyages to China and, like other sea captains, returned with silk, tea, and something called nankeen, a blue and white porcelain.

In 1793, the year Lucretia was born, the United States was still a young country. George Washington was just beginning his second term as president. Only ten years had passed since this nation had gained its independence. Leaders of the American Revolution had fought for life, liberty, and the pursuit of happiness, but their ideas of freedom and equal rights differed from those we have today. Freedom belonged only to whites and equal rights were shared only by white male property owners. Lucretia grew up to become a special person who would help change the way Americans thought and make this country a better place for all people. She convinced others that equal rights should be shared by all people, including women and African Americans. She helped put an end to slavery and provide men and women with equal opportunities. Her parents encouraged her to follow her Quaker beliefs and to stand up for what she believed was right. Like other Quakers, Lucretia opposed war, military service, and the use of violence. She tried to help create a world where peace and justice would overcome society's wrongs.

Lucretia's father liked adventure and, while at sea, his life was often in danger. Sometimes Thomas did not know if he would have enough food to last the journey or if he would be able to find his way home. He was a brave man and he passed on to his daughter his willingness to take risks.

Anna, Lucretia's mother, taught her daughter to be self-reliant. Since Nantucket men were so often away at sea, frequently for a year at a time, the women often had to raise the children and run the house by themselves. Anna used the wool she spun herself to sew clothes for the entire family. She baked cornbread to serve with fish and clams. She fixed corned beef and bacon, since these could be stored a long time without refrigeration. Anna liked to make her family's favorite dish—codfish and onions—and, for dessert, blackberry pudding.

Because of Thomas' frequent absences, Anna counted on Lucretia to help keep house and mind the other children. Although she was not the oldest, she was the one Anna counted on the most. Lucretia was a responsible child and a fast learner. But Lucretia could get quite angry if she thought something was unfair. She had an independent spirit which often led her to do as she pleased. Although Quakers were not supposed to make music, Lucretia was known on occasion to hum or sing. Her mother only teased her, "Oh, Lucretia, if thee was as far out of town as thee is out of tune, thee wouldn't get home tonight."

Anna set up a shop in one of the few rooms of their small house. There she sold the treasures Thomas brought back from his voyages. When Anna needed goods not found on the island, she went to "the continent"—the islanders' name for the mainland—and bartered. She exchanged the whaling oil her husband had given her and the candles which Lucretia and her sisters helped make for what she wanted.

While Anna was away, she left Lucretia in charge of both the shop and the children. When the children couldn't roast potatoes, they read and told stories. Quakers were not allowed to play cards, but they could hold spelling contests and play with jackstraws. Lucretia tried hard to take good care of her sisters and brother, and only sometimes lost her patience. Looking back, she once wrote, "I always loved the good, and in childhood tried to do right, praying for strength to overcome a naturally hasty temper."

Nantucket children spent many hours waiting for the return of a sea vessel and listening to the captain tell of his adventures. When the town crier was told that a ship was coming, he stood on the street corners to shout the news so everyone could hear. Whenever Lucretia heard the cry she climbed through the trapdoor to the platform, called a widow's walk, on the roof of her house. From here Lucretia could see miles away into the ocean and there await the ship returning home.

From the widow's walk Lucretia could see for miles.

When Lucretia was seven years old, her father set sail aboard his new ship, The Trial, in search of seal-skins to take on a trading venture to China. But he never made it to China. The Spaniards seized The Trial off the Pacific coast of South America and arrested Thomas for hunting seals in Spanish waters. They took him to Valparaiso in Chile, where they made him stand trial in the Spanish court. Thomas wrote Anna and the children to tell them what had happened, but the letters never reached them. Lucretia had no idea where her father was and wondered if she would ever see him again.

After a long dispute, the Spanish released Thomas, but did not return his vessel. Thomas had to walk across the huge chain of mountains called the Andes that stretches along the west coast of South America. He then traveled through Brazil to the Atlantic coast. There he convinced a ship's captain to take him on board and bring him home. Thomas found no way to send a message to his family. It was not until he walked in the door, months later, that they knew their waiting was over. Lucretia looked so much older that her father barely recognized her.

For the first few days Lucretia thought she must be dreaming. She had a hard time believing her father was really home. She needed to see him, touch him, and hear him to make sure he was real. As soon as she woke up in the morning and heard his voice, she rushed to his side. In the evenings she would listen to the tale of his adventures and learn the Spanish words he taught her. *Buenos dias* (which means good morning) and *buenas noches* (Spanish for good night) were two phrases she would not forget.

That was the last voyage Captain Coffin made. Lucretia's father promised never to leave home again.

Thomas Mott told the family of his adventures at sea.

To Boarding School

After Lucretia's eleventh birthday, Thomas and Anna told their children they were moving to Boston. Thomas, who had given up sea voyages, was going to become a merchant. Lucretia had never left the island before—not even for a short trip. She knew she would miss it and was determined not to forget the island, nor what she called "the Nantucket way" which the Quakers had taught her. This meant living simply and honestly, without placing too much emphasis on material things or possessions, but instead stressing the importance of the heart and mind.

Lucretia discovered the excitement of starting a new life in a new place, but her parents worried about her education. The Coffins believed that education was just as important for girls as it was for boys. However, in most day schools, public or private, girls were not taught the same subjects as boys. Boys studied Latin and Greek, and girls learned to cook and sew. Boys attended school all year long, but girls went to school only six months a year. Anna and Thomas talked it over and decided a girl could not receive an education equal to a boy's unless she went away to school. They had heard of Nine Partners, a Quaker boarding school in New York, where girls and boys were treated equally. This would be just the right school for Lucretia and her sister Eliza.

Nine Partners required their students to wear simple, practical clothing. They informed the parents, "If the clothing sent be not plain or require much washing it is to be returned or colored, or altered at the parent's expense. All the clothing sent to be strong and substantial." Girls needed to bring "one or two plain bonnets, one cloak, not silk, two gingham gowns suitable for the season, made plain, and three or four long checked aprons."

Nine Partners was such a great distance from Boston that Lucretia and Eliza remained there two years without returning home. The girls traveled by stagecoach for several days until they reached the hills near Poughkeepsie overlooking the Hudson River Valley. Lucretia and her sister lived and studied with the girls in one half of the long building. The boys were kept to the other side. The playground was divided by a fence which separated the girls and the boys. Only boys and girls who were close relatives could speak to each other over the fence. Lucretia and Eliza—who had no relatives at the school—were only allowed to play with the other girls.

Although the boys and girls were kept apart, they studied the same subjects, including English grammar, mathematics, and geography, and had to memorize long passages of poetry. Nine Partners exposed its students to new ideas. Lucretia was moved to hear an abolitionist denounce slavery. The speaker was the director of the school and his name was James Mott.

The Quaker school, Nine Partners, treated boys and girls equally.

James Mott and other abolitionists wanted to put an end to slavery by stopping the slave trade and freeing the slaves. After listening to James Mott, Lucretia read "An Essay on Slavery" by Thomas Clarkson, a British abolitionist. This account of the abuses suffered by slaves on their journey across the ocean so enraged Lucretia that it helped determine the course her life would take.

Quick to think and to reason, Lucretia was a good student, but she often got into trouble for talking out of turn. She hated to see anyone mistreated. Once she heard that a boy was being severely punished for no good reason. Lucretia and Eliza snuck into the boys' dormitory and found him locked in a closet. Knowing that he would be deprived of his supper, they tried hard not to be seen as they slipped slices of buttered bread under the door.

At school Lucretia soon became the best friend of James Mott's granddaughter, a girl named Sarah Mott. Once Lucretia accompanied Sarah home on a holiday and met the younger James Mott, Sarah's brother, who taught in the boys' division at Nine Partners. The following year, at age fifteen, Lucretia was asked to be an assistant teacher. She got to know James better and the two studied French together. James, tall with sandy hair and blue eyes, came across as shy and serious. Lucretia was just the opposite—short, with dark hair and hazel eyes, she was vivacious and impulsive. She laughed a lot, but, like James, also showed an earnestness and deep spiritual feeling. The two teachers fell in love.

Lucretia liked teaching and was made a regular teacher after one year as an assistant. But she became quite angry when she realized that a woman's salary was only half of what a male teacher was paid. "The unequal condition of woman impressed my mind," she later wrote. It was an injustice she would never forget.

While Lucretia was at Nine Partners, several changes had taken place in the Coffin family. Lucretia now had a new baby sister, named Martha. Her family had also decided to move to Philadelphia so that Thomas could take part in the family business. Thomas manufactured and sold cut-nails—a new form of nail with a blunt point. Lucretia and Eliza joined their family in their new home in 1809. James Mott moved to Philadelphia the following year to be closer to Lucretia. The two planned to get married and James took a job with his future father-in-law.

The Coffins met many other Friends in this "city of brotherly love," founded by William Penn, a Quaker from England. In 1681, the English king, Charles II, had granted Penn a charter to establish the "holy experiment," a colony in the New World where religious and political freedom would be granted. The following year Penn brought other Friends to the colony. Together they laid out the city of Philadelphia. These settlers befriended the Indians and later refused to take up arms during the Revolution. The Coffins had found a city where Friends felt at home, Quaker values were shared, and freedom of thought was encouraged.

Eliza and Lucretia slipped slices of buttered bread under the door.

A Quaker Marriage

I t was not long before James and Lucretia decided to "pass meeting" so they could get married. It was a Quaker custom for the couple to declare their intentions of marriage at the Friends' monthly meeting. Both sets of parents would give written permission and a committee of Friends would be appointed to determine whether or not the marriage was suitable for both the man and the woman. At the second monthly meeting—provided the committee reported that all was in order—the couple would be told they could proceed with the marriage.

Lucretia wore a pale gray dress to her wedding on April 10, 1811. They were married in the Quaker monthly meeting. James turned to Lucretia and, holding her hand, spoke these words, "I, James Mott, take thee, Lucretia Coffin, to be my wife, promising with divine assistance to be unto thee a loving and faithful husband so long as we both shall live." The eighteen year old Lucretia promised to be "a true and loving wife so long as we both shall live." The newly-weds then signed their names on the parchment which was their marriage certificate. The wedding ended with a period of worship and of silence.

Early in their marriage James and Lucretia shared a house with the Coffins while they saved money to buy a house of their own. James' grandfather reminded them that one's relationship with God was more important than material things. "May you experience this through life," he wrote them, "then whether prosperity shine upon you, or adversity be your lot, all will be well."

Lucretia took Grandfather Mott's words to heart and did not become too discouraged with their first business setbacks. "These trials in early life were not without their good effect in disciplining the mind and leading it to set a just estimate on worldly pleasures," Lucretia concluded. James left his father-in-law's business to work in a cotton mill. He later sold plows wholesale, but was never quite sure if his business would be successful.

James and Lucretia were married on April 10, 1811, at a Friends' monthly meeting.

James' grandfather wrote to them about the importance of God in their lives.

James and Lucretia soon had two children and decided to name them for Lucretia's parents. Anna was born in 1812, the year that war broke out between the United States and Great Britain. Two years later Thomas was born. James' business was not doing well and when Thomas turned one, Lucretia went back to teaching. She and a cousin, Rebecca Bunker, opened their own school with the help of Friends from Pine Street Meetinghouse. They took in ten students, but by the end of the year they had forty.

In April 1817, both Lucretia and her three year old son Thomas were struck with high fevers. Lucretia recovered, but her little son did not. Both parents were heartbroken by his death. The following months were the most painful either one of them had experienced. Lucretia missed her son terribly and became ill, but her faith in God helped her through her suffering. Religious thoughts preoccupied more and more of her waking hours. Years later Lucretia would tell her grandchildren that her grief at her son's death turned her mind toward becoming a preacher in the Society of Friends.

Friends believe that the spirit of God can be found in every human being and that each person is guided by an "inner light." When Friends gather at meetings for worship, they do not follow an established service or ritual. Instead they observe periods of silence and speak when the spirit moves them. Simplicity and moderation are their guiding principles. In the eighteenth and nineteenth centuries this was evident in their dress—the plain gray clothes and the lack of frills.

The more Lucretia thought about becoming a minister, the more she studied books written by Quakers. After a new baby girl named Maria was born, she rocked her to sleep with a book in her hand. The works of William Penn inspired Lucretia to keep reading about Quakers. She learned about George Fox who had founded the Society of Friends in the middle of the seventeenth century. An Englishman and a passionate speaker, Fox opposed many of the religious traditions, services and rituals in the English church. He and his followers also refused to take oaths, use weapons, or serve in armies. Although Fox was often arrested and put in prison for his beliefs, he did not stop preaching.

Lucretia, a thoughtful woman with strong convictions, was also a good speaker. Quakers began to recognize that she had the special gift of ministry. In 1821 Lucretia was selected to become a minister of the Society of Friends. Lucretia's calling would lead her to give sermons in Philadelphia, as well as many parts of the United States and England.

A boy, the second Thomas Coffin Mott, was born in 1823; a girl, Elizabeth, two years later; and one more girl, Martha, in 1828. Lucretia's family teased her because she still kept a book at the foot of the cradle. Lucretia was influenced not only by Quaker writings, but by a book titled *Vindication of the Rights of Woman.* In this work, published in 1792, a woman named Mary Wollstonecraft dared for the first time to demand equal rights for women. As Lucretia read, she developed new ideas that would change her outlook on the role of women, influence her sermons, and help transform the status of women throughout the country.

Lucretia first read of equal rights for women as she rocked baby Martha to sleep.

Joining the Abolitionists

European slave traders had brought the first African slaves to the New World in 1517. For over three hundred years they kept on coming until the slaves numbered more than four million. In the American south they helped grow tobacco, sugar, and cotton on large plantations. The Quakers were the first to oppose slavery, speaking out in Pennsylvania in 1688. The English Quakers started a strong anti-slavery movement in 1783. Fourteen years later both Britain and the United States abolished the slave trade. In 1834 Britain freed the slaves in its Caribbean colonies. But American abolitionists, as those who opposed slavery were called, had fought without success. When Lucretia was called to the ministry, she became a formidable opponent of slavery.

In 1826, James Mott and forty Friends formed the Philadelphia Free Produce Society to encourage people not to buy goods produced by slave labor, but to buy "free produce" instead. "Free produce" would involve only the labor of free men. James and Lucretia decided they would stop using goods produced by slave labor, including cotton, sugar, and molasses. They would only buy candy for their children in stores selling "free produce." James, who had been working in the cotton business, chose to give it up rather than work with the product of slave labor. James started yet a new venture, this time in the wool business, where he remained until his retirement.

The older the children grew, the more Lucretia traveled to preach at Quaker meetings. Sometimes with James, sometimes without, Lucretia gave sermons throughout New York and New England and as far south as Virginia. In one seventy-day journey, she and her husband covered 2,400 miles, most of it by stagecoach, and they attended seventy-one meetings. Lucretia, who never got tired, spoke at each one. James recognized Lucretia's talent for preaching. Although he shared her beliefs and the desire to work for her causes, he did not feel driven to speak.

Lucretia and James traveled 2,400 miles to attend seventy-one meetings.

In 1830, Lucretia met William Lloyd Garrison, the fiery abolitionist who would become her close friend. This young writer saw that Lucretia shared his convictions. He admired her intelligence and her willingness to help others. When Garrison started to publish *The Liberator,* the first newspaper to call for the unconditional abolition of slavery, Lucretia took an avid interest. In 1833, Garrison called the first meeting of a newly formed association, the Anti-Slavery Society. Both Lucretia and James were by his side. Women were permitted to attend, but did not sign the petition that was drawn up at the meeting. The petition called for an end to slavery as well as prejudice. Some well-known abolitionists found the document too strongly worded and refused to sign it. Although it was uncommon for women to address a public group outside of a Quaker meeting, Lucretia's voice rang out. "Right principles are stronger than great names. If our principles are right, why should we be cowards?" Lucretia demanded. "Why should we wait for those who never have had the courage to maintain the inalienable rights of the slave?"

A few days later Lucretia gathered together a group of black and white women to form the Female Anti-Slavery Society. She served as president for many years. Members called her a "wise counselor" and an "active worker." They admired her for her convictions and her style. When she spoke she would win over her audience with her forceful voice and her keen sense of humor. This society held its first Anti-Slavery Fair to raise money for the abolitionist cause. Although the Quaker members opposed fairs, Lucretia persuaded several to take part. She enlisted the help of many Friends as well as her older children. Thomas pitched in to sweep floors and the girls took charge of several booths. The fair became an annual event and raised enough money to print anti-slavery pamphlets, hire lecturers, and help start a school for black children.

It was uncommon for women to address a public group outside of a Quaker meeting.

The crowd left the hall in flames.

Abolitionists often had trouble finding places to hold their meetings. In December of 1836, Lucretia and James started to raise money for a new hall in Philadelphia where abolitionists could hold their meetings. They raised forty thousand dollars and the building began. By 1838, the new Pennsylvania Hall, with an auditorium that would seat three thousand, was completed and the Anti-Slavery Convention of American Women was scheduled to start its first session on May 14. Anti-abolitionists, angered by the presence of black women in the Hall, wanted to stop the proceedings. They met outside the convention in an attempt to disrupt the meetings. The mayor requested that black women not attend the meeting, but Lucretia urged them to ignore his request. By nightfall of the third day, a mob of 17,000 gathered outside Pennsylvania Hall. They forced their way into the building and set fire to the wooden benches. Pennsylvania Hall burned to the ground.

As the crowd left the hall in flames, the anti-abolitionists threatened to attack the Motts' house. Lucretia sent the younger children to a friend's house and sat down with her husband to await the rioters. Many Friends rushed over to Lucretia's house to advise her to stay calm. "It was really amusing and somewhat ludicrous to hear them, all tremulous with agitation, gravely counseling her to keep cool, and avoid undue excitement;" a guest staying with the Motts wrote, "while she all the time was as calm as a summer evening, perfectly composed, and with all her faculties entirely at command." The rioters set out down the street in search of the Motts' house. The Motts' son Thomas burst inside the house yelling "They're coming!" But a friend of the Motts, in order to protect them, joined the mob, screamed "On to the Motts!" and then led them down the wrong street. As the night grew darker, the crowd lost all hope of finding the Motts.

After the burning of Pennsylvania Hall, William Garrison called together a group to establish the New England Non-Resistance Society. In its Declaration of Sentiments the group rejected not only force, but all government based on force. Lucretia was unable to attend the first meeting, but did travel by stagecoach to Boston to attend the first anniversary meeting in 1839. At this meeting members discussed nonresistance and agreed that force should not be used to bring about change. They also talked about the role of parents in educating children. How could parents teach children to find non-violent solutions to problems if they themselves used force to discipline their children? Should paddling be used as a form of punishment? What other means did parents have of helping their children understand what was right and wrong? Could children learn to obey through love and not through fear?

Some who attended the Non-Resistance Society's meeting severely criticized Lucretia. "She spends too much time with the 'World's People'," one Quaker charged. "She adopts causes but is not close enough to God," another said. But none of these remarks stopped Lucretia from preaching about abolition or nonresistance as she went from one Friends' meeting to another.

In 1840 the British organized the World's Anti-Slavery Convention and invited delegates from around the world. The American Anti-Slavery Convention chose Lucretia and James to be two of their four delegates. A family friend and distant relative, who was sympathetic to the cause, helped finance the Motts' trip. On May 7, 1840 James and Lucretia set sail for England on the Roscoe. Although occasionally seasick, Lucretia enjoyed the voyage and took great pleasure in her conversations with the other passengers.

The Motts arrived in Liverpool three weeks later and traveled to London by stagecoach, stopping at sights along the way. Not until they attended the opening session of the convention did Lucretia realize that women were to be excluded from the proceedings. Told to leave the floor, the women were escorted to a balcony where they had to sit behind a bar. Lucretia was outraged. So was another American, the twenty-five year old Elizabeth Cady Stanton, who had come to England on her honeymoon to accompany her husband to the convention. Lucretia and Elizabeth became fast friends. William Garrison, angered that women were not allowed to participate, joined them behind the bar in the balcony. Although formally excluded from the convention, Lucretia was by no means ignored. Her reputation had spread across the Atlantic and many were eager to meet her. She preached outside the convention and her words inspired those who came to listen. She herself was moved to hear the now white-haired Thomas Clarkson, whose writing had inspired her back at Nine Partners School.

On her trip Lucretia met and influenced many, but the most important event for her was meeting Elizabeth Cady Stanton. Before Lucretia and Elizabeth parted, they vowed to work together to promote equal rights for women.

The transatlantic trip took three weeks.

William Garrison joined the women in the balcony.

After the Motts returned home, Lucretia fought even harder for the causes in which she believed. Invitations to speak poured in from all over the Northeast and Midwest. When she traveled, strangers often recognized her and stopped her on the street to speak to her. Lucretia did not read from a prepared text, but when she stood to speak, the words never failed to come. Although a small woman, she had a commanding presence and a tremendous capacity to capture her audience, sometimes transfixing them with the power of her speech.

Lucretia found time for her public speaking by cutting down on her domestic chores. "One secret of her accomplishing so much, was her power of discriminating between the necessary and the unnecessary duties of housekeeping," her granddaughter observed. "The essentials were always attended to, but the non-essentials—the self-imposed labors under which so many women struggle —were left to look after themselves." Lucretia explained it this way: "Being fond of reading, I omitted much unnecessary stitching and ornamental work in the sewing for my family, so that I might have more time for this indulgence, and for the improvement of the mind." Lucretia was both frugal and efficient. She kept her desires simple and she made good use of her time. Having learned never to waste a moment, she always brought her knitting to her meetings.

In January 1843, Lucretia, now fifty years old, asked to speak to the United States Congress. She was granted permission—provided she remain silent on the subject of slavery. She refused. She spoke instead at the Unitarian Church, to an audience which included over forty congress-men and the well-known thinker and writer, Ralph Waldo Emerson. Lucretia left the church all the more determined to talk to the president about the emancipation of the slaves. She and James walked to the White House and asked to speak with the president. President John Tyler agreed to meet with them and together the three discussed their views on slavery. At the end of their visit the president was charmed by Lucretia. He even admired her strong character, but he remained unpersuaded. Lucretia left, disappointed that the president would not take immediate action. "Our hopes of success must not rest on those in power, but on the common people, whose servants they are," she concluded.

"...all men and women are created equal...", Lucretia told the women at Seneca Falls.

Speaking Out on Women's Rights

I n the summer of 1848, Lucretia and James traveled to New York to see several settlements of escaped slaves. They also visited with Lucretia's sister and brother-in-law, Martha and David Wright, in Auburn, New York. On this trip Lucretia once again met Elizabeth Cady Stanton and she was reminded of one of Elizabeth's letters. "The more I think on the present condition of woman, the more am I oppressed with the reality of her degradation" she had written. "The laws of our country, how unjust are they! our customs, how vicious!" Lucretia, Elizabeth, Lucretia's sister Martha, and two other Quakers talked over tea and together they decided to call a Woman's Rights Convention. It was to be held in the nearby town of Seneca Falls, where Elizabeth lived. A notice they placed in the *Seneca County Courier* said the convention would "discuss the social, civil, and religious conditions and rights of woman."

The organizers opened the doors to the convention at 10 a.m. on Wednesday, July 19 at the Wesleyan Chapel. Once the meeting started, Lucretia became what one observer called its "guiding spirit." Lucretia and Elizabeth had written a Declaration of Sentiments based on the Declaration of Independence, but making several key changes. They began with: "We hold these truths to be self-evident: that all men and women are created equal." The Declaration, read out loud many times during the convention, called for equal rights for women to obtain a college education, pursue a career, own property and vote. One hundred men and women signed the declaration.

Newspapers all around the nation ridiculed the Woman's Rights Convention. Reporters everywhere poked fun at Lucretia Mott and Elizabeth Cady Stanton. But all the press coverage aroused readers' interest in women's rights and inspired women to hold their own conventions.

The following year Lucretia gave a speech called "Discourse on Woman." Lucretia said equal treatment was something women should not "ask for as a favor," but "claim as right." She demanded equal education, including the establishment of girls' high schools—in a state which then had none. She pointed out that women must pay taxes, support the government, and obey its laws, and yet cannot vote. This she called "political slavery." She also explained that although a single woman could own property, once she married, she lost that right and what she owned became her husband's property. "The law is a disgrace to any civilized nation," she concluded. She proclaimed that doors to different professions, such as medicine, should be opened to women and that women's salaries should equal those of men. This discourse was recorded by a reporter in Philadelphia and published as a pamphlet. Twenty years later it was reprinted and distributed in England.

Lucretia Mott was the oldest leader in the struggle for equal rights in this country. Younger women in the movement, including Elizabeth Cady Stanton, Susan B. Anthony, and Lucy Stone, turned to Lucretia for advice. Lucretia gave them all support and encouragement.

Room for One More

T he Motts' red brick townhouse on Arch Street in Philadelphia was always full. This large house could accommodate Lucretia and James' children and their growing families. Martha moved in with her husband and baby. Thomas and Maria and their families lived on farms outside the city in the summer, but spent the winters with James and Lucretia. With visitors coming to call, it was not unusual for thirty people to sit down to dinner. Anyone interested in abolition or women's rights always felt welcome at the Motts. Their hospitality was legendary.

Sojourner Truth, the freed slave who, although she could not read or write, was a powerful speaker for emancipation, visited often. So did Frederick Douglass, an abolitionist and former slave, and James Miller McKim, another abolitionist and close friend of Lucretia, with whom she liked to discuss at great length the issues of the day. William Garrison, the uncompromising abolitionist, also turned up frequently at the Motts. He knew there was always room for one more. Lucretia opened her doors to the poor as well. The family suggested she place two chairs just within the doorway of the Mott home to be dubbed "beggars' chairs." Lucretia served her guests her favorite dishes: milk biscuits, scrapple made from pork and corn mush, and all sorts of puddings—blackberry, lemon, or plum.

In 1850, the passage of the Fugitive Slave Law made it more difficult for slaves to obtain their freedom by traveling north. This law provided for the return of escaped slaves from one state to another. If slaves were caught trying to escape, they would not be allowed to testify or

The Motts' hospitality was legendary.

Passengers on the underground railroad traveled by night, following the North Star.

have a trial by jury. Individuals who helped fugitive slaves would be punished. The law angered many and made them more determined to find a means for the slaves to escape. A secret system which became known as the "underground railroad" was developed to assist the runaway slaves. Harriet Tubman and other former slaves, abolitionists, and many Quakers provided a refuge for the slaves as they made their way north. The slaves or "passengers" traveled by night following the North Star on different routes which were called "lines." They stopped along the way at "stations" or "depots" and were helped by "conductors" or "station masters." It is estimated that 75,000 passengers reached freedom on the underground railroad. Because the slaves moved secretly, an exact number is not known.

The underground railroad brought many slaves through Philadelphia. Runaway slaves found a safe place to hide at the Motts' home, which became a station on the underground railroad. One of the passengers they met was a two hundred pound man who had escaped from Richmond, Virginia, hidden in a box and shipped north. The man remained seated in the box, two feet long, twenty three inches wide, and three feet high, for twenty-four hours. When he climbed out of the box in Philadelphia, he was ready for breakfast.

In 1856, James and Lucretia left their city home and moved to a farmhouse six miles outside Philadelphia, which they called Roadside. They continued to take in passengers on the underground railroad. Lucretia warmed the parlor with a Franklin stove and cut down the shrubs outside to gain more light. Their new house was cheerful and cozy. Life here was not quite as busy as it had been in the city, but the Motts' house still remained a gathering place and a refuge for reformists.

John Brown had the freedom of the slaves on his mind and in his heart, right up to the moment of his hanging.

John Brown and the Civil War

The abolitionist, John Brown, ran a station on the underground railroad at Harpers Ferry in the mountains of West Virginia. He hoped to make the town safe for fugitive slaves. On October 16, 1859, he gathered together a band of anti-slavery men, weapons and ammunition. The group gained control of the armory at Harpers Ferry and took sixty men as hostages. John Brown hoped that escaped slaves would join him and form an army to free the slaves. Two days later John Brown was captured and wounded; ten of his men, including two of his sons, were killed. The rebellious leader was tried, convicted, and hanged. The trial made headlines. Northerners and southerners debated what he had done, some calling him a madman and others a martyr and "angel of light." John Brown's trial signaled to the nation that the issue of slavery needed to be addressed.

While John Brown stood trial, his wife Mary found shelter with the Motts. Although Lucretia thought John Brown was wrong to use violence, her heart went out to both John and Mary and she wanted to comfort Mary as best she could. Later, Mary Brown brought her husband's body by train through Philadelphia on her way to the Adirondacks for the burial. At the memorial meeting in Philadelphia, Lucretia's voice was heard crying out against the sin of slavery.

Lucretia spoke so vehemently against slavery that a friend accused her of being "the most belligerent Quaker" he had ever met. Lucretia answered "for it is not John Brown the soldier we praise, it is John Brown the moral hero...I have no idea because I am a Non-Resister of submitting tamely to injustice inflicted either on me or on the slave. I will oppose it with all the moral power with which I am endowed. I am no advocate of passivity. Quakerism as I understand it does not mean quietism. The early Friends were agitators, disturbers of the peace, and were more obnoxious in their day to charges which are now so freely made than we are."

Lucretia had an eye for injustice; she was not going to sit still and let the world pass her by just because she was a Quaker and would not use violence. She was going to fight injustice too; only her weapons were different. Because of her example no one could accuse a pacifist of being passive. "Truth for authority, not authority for truth" became her motto. Lucretia believed men and women should be guided by truth and not assume that those who have authority, speak the truth.

On April 10, 1861, shortly after President Abraham Lincoln took office, Lucretia and James celebrated their fiftieth anniversary. Their large family, including the newest great grandchild, and several hundred friends gathered together at Roadside for the joyful occasion. Only two days later an event occurred which changed the course of American history, dividing its people, turning brother against brother. With the first shots fired on Fort Sumter in South Carolina, the Civil War began and brought to a violent climax deep-rooted tensions between the North and South. Eleven southern states seceded to form the Confederacy; the Union fought to win them back.

The Union army leased a large field neighboring Roadside and used it as a training camp for black soldiers. They called it Camp William Penn. Although Lucretia had fought so long to end slavery, she did not believe the country should resort to war. She condemned war and yet she made friends with the soldiers. Lucretia could watch the regiments drill from her parlor window. Sometimes she came outside to pass out gingerbread to the men. She often asked herself "Why should the young and beautiful be swept away?" She wanted to put an end to slavery, but she did not believe war was the answer. Lucretia was invited to speak to the soldiers and, on July 12, 1863, walked over to the camp. The commanding officer asked her to stand on a drum so she could be seen by the six hundred soldiers who had marched in front of her. She offered them hope and shared with them her faith that the time would come when war would be no more.

Lucretia watched as family members, friends, neighbors and abolitionists who had once adopted principles of non-resistance, now joined the army. Even Lucretia's Quaker son-in-law, Edward Davis, enlisted. Lucretia worried when she heard the news that her sister Martha's son was wounded at the battle of Gettysburg. This bloody battle fought in July 1863 marked the turning point of the war as the North took the lead over the South. But the fighting continued for almost two years.

In March 1865, Abraham Lincoln gave his second inaugural address to the people and spoke these words, "With malice toward none; with charity for all; with firmness in the right, as God gives us to see the right, let us strive on to finish the work we are in; to bind up the nation's wounds." On April 9, the Confederacy surrendered to the Union. The Civil War came to a close with six hundred thousand dead on both sides. Six days later, Lincoln died from an assassin's bullet. Lucretia wrote her sister, "When a great calamity has befallen the nation, we want the sun to be darkened, and the moon not to give her light."

Lucretia offered the soldiers hope and spoke of a time when there would no longer be war.

Roadside

The passage of the thirteenth amendment to the Constitution abolished slavery throughout the land. The slaves were free at last, but much work remained to be done to rebuild the country and establish a nation where equal rights would be shared by all. Lucretia and James both knew the real battle lay ahead.

When Lucretia and James traveled by horse-drawn car between Roadside and Philadelphia, they noticed that black people were often not allowed to ride inside passenger cars, but had to ride out in the open. Lucretia, angry and indignant, asked herself why she should sit while others had to stand. She would leave the passenger car and stand in the area reserved for blacks as a protest to this segregation. Lucretia and James joined the Friends Association for the Aid and Elevation of the Freedmen which was trying to secure equal rights for the former slaves. They organized a committee to "investigate the exclusion of the people of color from the passenger cars." In 1867 the Pennsylvania legislature passed a law forbidding discrimination in public transportation.

Lucretia helped establish The Stephen Smith Home, a nursing home in Philadelphia for people of color. She made scrapple and baked pies for the residents. She raised money to support schools for freedmen, established by women who had come to Roadside to visit her. From her windows at Roadside she watched houses being built where she had seen soldiers train at what was once Camp William Penn. Blacks and whites came here to live in one of the first integrated communities, named La Mott in honor of Lucretia.

The Cause of Peace

T he Quaker Alfred Love was called a conscientious objector because he would not fight in the war and refused to be drafted. He also would not hire someone to go to war in his place, as other Quakers had done. Lucretia had gotten to know him during his draft hearings. When Alfred Love called a meeting of a new group, the Universal Peace Union, in 1866, the Motts participated. All who attended wanted to remake society in the spirit of love and create a world in which war had no part.

Members of the Universal Peace Union favored an international court of justice so that countries would no longer resort to war to resolve their differences. Instead they would send representatives to meet, discuss issues, and reach non-violent solutions. Members of the Universal Peace Union opposed using tax dollars for the military, training young men to be soldiers, and glorifying war. They promoted a pacifist education and denounced physical punishment, military drill and warlike toys.

After the first meeting Alfred Love invited those who were interested to found local branches. James and Lucretia formed the Pennsylvania Peace Society. The principles of the Pennsylvania Peace Society—like those of the Universal Peace Union—were ones in which James and Lucretia as Quakers had always believed. They had brought up their children to share similar views. The Peace Society gave them the opportunity to make their opinions known to a larger public. The ideas were not new to James and Lucretia, but now they had a greater opportunity to influence others.

James' dying words were of peace, kindness and love between all men.

In 1867, James Mott spoke at a Friends' Meeting in Abington near Philadelphia on the principles of peace and the importance of the home. "Everyone will admit that peace is better than war—that harmony and good feeling in a neighborhood are much better than strife and contention. We all feel that the same is true of nations," he said. He then asked, "How are we going to bring about a feeling of peace, kindness, and love in the community generally, so that we shall be able to uproot all war and bitterness? I do not know any better way than to begin at home with our children. I do not know of any better or more certain way to bring peace on earth," James added "than for each to see that we have it within ourselves, and then cultivate it in the minds of little children."

These were the last public words that James spoke before he died early the following year. Lucretia, now seventy-five, would not forget his words, nor neglect the cause to which both of them had devoted their lives.

After James' death Lucretia remained closer to home and attended fewer public meetings. She gave up the running of the house and left this to the children who had joined her at Roadside. But she still cooked certain favorite dishes: the Nantucket blackberry pudding, the corn soup and the mince pie. Lucretia, who had always been thrifty, continued to make the colorful "hit or miss carpets" out of household rags she had saved, a craft she had learned on Nantucket. Lucretia cut the pieces, sewed them, and nailed the carpets to the floor. She also insisted on helping her children and grandchildren with their carpets.

In the fall of 1869, Lucretia attended the opening of the Quaker college at Swarthmore. Lucretia came to represent James who had served on the Board of Managers and helped establish the college. She brought with her two oak trees from Roadside to plant on the campus as a tribute to her husband's interest in education. Recalling the first time she had laid eyes on James at Nine Partners School, Lucretia thought of how much had changed since then. Sixty years ago Nine Partners was one of the rare schools to offer girls and boys equal education at the high school level. Now Swarthmore College was about to open its doors to both young men and women. The college, named for the home of George Fox, founder of the Society of Friends, would promote co-education, Quaker ideals and the highest level of instruction.

Lucretia, now President of the Pennsylvania Peace Society, addressed the Abington Peace Meeting in 1875 on "A Faithful Testimony against Bearing Arms." Frail with age and weighing less than one hundred pounds, Lucretia nevertheless delivered her speech with a clear and strong voice: "During the late war some of our young men were tempted to join the army; many of those whom I have conversed with since their return say they are more opposed to war since they have seen its terrible evils." She continued, "We all love Peace in our best moments; it is a part of the divine nature implanted in us. I believe little children have this feeling, but parents and care-takers often commit the great mistake of teaching them that they must not bear insults; then, too, they are taught by their surroundings, by the pomp and parade of the military, they are attracted by the music, and in many ways the terrible nature of war, which is so revolting to every refined feeling, is concealed and they are made to see it as something to glory in."

Lucretia, now well into her eighties, had become set in her ways and developed a few eccentricities. She refused to carry an umbrella; she often ate only peas for dinner; she insisted on traveling alone; she never used stationery, but wrote her letters on scraps of paper or backs of envelopes. She refused to buy anything new; instead she mended everything. More than once she was seen catching a stray feather and putting it back into a pillow. Still eager to change the world, she never retired from public speaking.

At the age of eighty-seven she suffered from a brief illness. "There never was a sick person who required so little done for her," the niece who cared for her said. She asked only that her great grandson sing to her in the morning. When he finished his song, she would call him to her bedside and hand him a penny from under her pillow. Then on November 11, 1880, when all her children and grandchildren had been called together to Roadside to be with her for the last time, Lucretia died.

Several thousand came to witness Lucretia's burial. The ceremony was conducted in a simple fashion and in profound silence. Lucretia was placed in the ground next to her husband.

Only one voice cried out, "Will no one say anything?"

Another answered, "Who can speak? The preacher is dead."

Frederick Douglass, the orator who was once a slave and a visitor in Lucretia's home, found Lucretia Mott to be one of the greatest preachers he had ever heard. "My heart has always been made better," he said, "and my spirit raised by her words; and in speaking thus for myself I am sure I am expressing the experience of thousands." Frederick Douglass believed that "when the true history of the anti-slavery cause shall be written, women will occupy a large space in its pages. Foremost among these noble American women," he wrote, "in point of clearness of vision, breadth of understanding, fullness of knowledge, weight of character, and widespread influence, was Lucretia Mott."

Lucretia made "hit or miss carpets" out of scraps she saved.

In the United States Capitol, we can see the statues of Elizabeth Cady Stanton, Susan B. Anthony, and Lucretia Mott.

For Justice

L ucretia Mott was an early pioneer, one of the first in the United States working to abolish slavery, to provide equal rights for men and women of all races, and to create a more peaceful world. By the time of her death in 1880 much progress had been made, but her work was unfinished. Although the fourteenth and fifteenth amendments to the Constitution granted equal rights to blacks, not all blacks could exercise those rights. Women could not vote and would not gain that right until 1920. World leaders would continue to talk of peace, but resort to war. The twentieth century would see U.S. involvement in two world wars, as well as wars in Korea, Vietnam, and the Persian Gulf. And yet there are still many who continue the struggle for equal rights, many who continue to protest war. Today's Quakers, represented by the American Friends Service Committee, are still passionately committed to teaching young and old about peace and justice. Lucretia Mott's spirit lives on, a reminder to us all of the tremendous work to be done.

Today in the crypt of the United States Capitol, we can see statues of three women, Elizabeth Cady Stanton, Susan B. Anthony, and Lucretia Mott. Lucretia's face shows determination and at the same time peacefulness—her Quaker heritage. She would want to be remembered not only for the causes to which she dedicated her life, but also for the gifts she inherited from her parents, her father's willingness to take risks and her mother's strong and independent spirit. She stood up for what she believed in, and no matter how unpopular the cause, Lucretia Mott was always a Friend of Justice.

48